A VILLAGE LIFE

ALSO BY LOUISE GLÜCK

POETRY

Firstborn

The House on Marshland

Descending Figure

The Triumph of Achilles

Ararat

The Wild Iris

Meadowlands

Vita Nova

The Seven Ages

Averno

ESSAYS

Proofs and Theories: Essays on Poetry

A VILLAGE LIFE

LOUISE GLÜCK

FARRAR, STRAUS AND GIROUX

NEW YORK

FARRAR, STRAUS AND GIROUX
18 West 18th Street, New York 10011

Distributed in Canada by D&M Publishers, Inc.
Printed in the United States of America
First edition, 2009

Grateful acknowledgment is made to the following publications, in
which some of these poems first appeared: *The American Scholar, The
Electronic Poetry Review, The New Yorker, The Paris Review, Poetry, Slate,
The Threepenny Review, The Yale Review.*

Library of Congress Cataloging-in-Publication Data
Glück, Louise, 1943–
    A village life / Louise Glück.— 1st ed.
      p. cm.
    ISBN-13: 978-0-374-28374-2 (alk. paper)
    ISBN-10: 0-374-28374-5 (alk. paper)
    I. Title.

PS3557.L8V55 2009
811'.54—dc22

                                        2008049218

Designed by Gretchen Achilles

www.fsgbooks.com

10   9   8   7   6   5   4   3   2   1

TO JAMES LONGENBACH

CONTENTS

TWILIGHT 3

PASTORAL 4

TRIBUTARIES 6

NOON 8

BEFORE THE STORM 10

SUNSET 12

IN THE CAFÉ 13

IN THE PLAZA 16

DAWN 17

FIRST SNOW 19

EARTHWORM 20

AT THE RIVER 21

A CORRIDOR 24

FATIGUE 25

BURNING LEAVES 26

WALKING AT NIGHT 27

VIA DELLE OMBRE 29

HUNTERS 31

A SLIP OF PAPER 32

BATS 34

BURNING LEAVES 35

MARCH 36

A NIGHT IN SPRING 39

HARVEST 41

CONFESSION 43

MARRIAGE 45

PRIMAVERA 46

FIGS   47

AT THE DANCE   50

SOLITUDE   52

EARTHWORM   53

OLIVE TREES   54

SUNRISE   57

A WARM DAY   59

BURNING LEAVES   61

CROSSROADS   62

BATS   63

ABUNDANCE   64

MIDSUMMER   65

THRESHING   67

A VILLAGE LIFE   69

Note   72

A VILLAGE LIFE

TWILIGHT

All day he works at his cousin's mill,
so when he gets home at night, he always sits at this one window,
sees one time of day, twilight.
There should be more time like this, to sit and dream.
It's as his cousin says:
Living—living takes you away from sitting.

In the window, not the world but a squared-off landscape
representing the world. The seasons change,
each visible only a few hours a day.
Green things followed by golden things followed by whiteness—
abstractions from which come intense pleasures,
like the figs on the table.

At dusk, the sun goes down in a haze of red fire between two poplars.
It goes down late in summer—sometimes it's hard to stay awake.

Then everything falls away.
The world for a little longer
is something to see, then only something to hear,
crickets, cicadas.
Or to smell sometimes, aroma of lemon trees, of orange trees.
Then sleep takes this away also.

But it's easy to give things up like this, experimentally,
for a matter of hours.

I open my fingers—
I let everything go.

Visual world, language,
rustling of leaves in the night,
smell of high grass, of woodsmoke.

I let it go, then I light the candle.

PASTORAL

The sun rises over the mountain.
Sometimes there's mist
but the sun's behind it always
and the mist isn't equal to it.
The sun burns its way through,
like the mind defeating stupidity.
When the mist clears, you see the meadow.

No one really understands
the savagery of this place,
the way it kills people for no reason,
just to keep in practice.

So people flee—and for a while, away from here,
they're exuberant, surrounded by so many choices—

But no signal from earth
will ever reach the sun. Thrash
against that fact, you are lost.

When they come back, they're worse.
They think they failed in the city,
not that the city doesn't make good its promises.
They blame their upbringing: youth ended and they're back,
silent, like their fathers.
Sundays, in summer, they lean against the wall of the clinic,
smoking cigarettes. When they remember,
they pick flowers for their girlfriends—

It makes the girls happy.
They think it's pretty here, but they miss the city, the afternoons
filled with shopping and talking, what you do
when you have no money...

To my mind, you're better off if you stay;
that way, dreams don't damage you.
At dusk, you sit by the window. Wherever you live,
you can see the fields, the river, realities
on which you cannot impose yourself—

To me, it's safe. The sun rises; the mist
dissipates to reveal
the immense mountain. You can see the peak,
how white it is, even in summer. And the sky's so blue,
punctuated with small pines
like spears—

When you got tired of walking
you lay down in the grass.
When you got up again, you could see for a moment where you'd been,
the grass was slick there, flattened out
into the shape of a body. When you looked back later,
it was as though you'd never been there at all.

Midafternoon, midsummer. The fields go on forever,
peaceful, beautiful.
Like butterflies with their black markings,
the poppies open.

All the roads in the village unite at the fountain.
Avenue of Liberty, Avenue of the Acacia Trees—
The fountain rises at the center of the plaza;
on sunny days, rainbows in the piss of the cherub.

In summer, couples sit at the pool's edge.
There's room in the pool for many reflections—
the plaza's nearly empty, the acacia trees don't get this far.
And the Avenue of Liberty is barren and austere; its image
doesn't crowd the water.

Interspersed with the couples, mothers with their younger children.
Here's where they come to talk to one another, maybe
meet a young man, see if there's anything left of their beauty.
When they look down, it's a sad moment: the water isn't encouraging.

The husbands are off working, but by some miracle
all the amorous young men are always free—
they sit at the edge of the fountain, splashing their sweethearts
with fountain water.

Around the fountain, there are clusters of metal tables.
This is where you sit when you're old,
beyond the intensities of the fountain.
The fountain is for the young, who still want to look at themselves.
Or for the mothers, who need to keep their children diverted.

In good weather, a few old people linger at the tables.
Life is simple now: one day cognac, one day coffee and a cigarette.
To the couples, it's clear who's on the outskirts of life, who's at the center.

The children cry, they sometimes fight over toys.
But the water's there, to remind the mothers that they love these children;
that for them to drown would be terrible.

The mothers are tired constantly, the children are always fighting,
the husbands at work or angry. No young man comes.
The couples are like an image from some faraway time, an echo coming
very faint from the mountains.

They're alone at the fountain, in a dark well.
They've been exiled by the world of hope,
which is the world of action,
but the world of thought hasn't as yet opened to them.
When it does, everything will change.

Darkness is falling, the plaza empties.
The first leaves of autumn litter the fountain.
The roads don't gather here anymore;
the fountain sends them away, back into the hills they came from.

Avenue of Broken Faith, Avenue of Disappointment,
Avenue of the Acacia Trees, of Olive Trees,
the wind filling with silver leaves,

Avenue of Lost Time, Avenue of Liberty that ends in stone,
not at the field's edge but at the foot of the mountain.

NOON

They're not grown up—more like a boy and girl, really.
School's over. It's the best part of the summer, when it's still beginning—
the sun's shining, but the heat isn't intense yet.
And freedom hasn't gotten boring.

So you can spend the whole day, all of it, wandering in the meadow.
The meadow goes on indefinitely, and the village keeps getting more and
    more faint—

It seems a strange position, being very young.
They have this thing everyone wants and they *don't* want—
but they want to keep it anyway; it's all they can trade on.

When they're by themselves like this, these are the things they talk about.
How time for them doesn't race.
It's like the reel breaking at the movie theater. They stay anyway—
mainly, they just don't want to leave. But till the reel is fixed,
the old one just gets popped back in,
and all of a sudden you're back to long ago in the movie—
the hero hasn't even met the heroine. He's still at the factory,
he hasn't begun to go bad. And she's wandering around the docks, already bad.
But she never meant it to happen. She was good, then it happened to her,
like a bag pulled over her head.

The sky's completely blue, so the grass is dry.
They'll be able to sit with no trouble.
They sit, they talk about everything—then they eat their picnic.
They put the food on the blanket, so it stays clean.
They've always done it this way; they take the grass themselves.

The rest—how two people can lie down on the blanket—
they know about it but they're not ready for it.
They know people who've done it, as a kind of game or trial—
then you say, no, wrong time, I think I'll just keep being a child.

But your body doesn't listen. It knows everything now,
it says you're not a child, you haven't been a child for a long time.

Their thinking is, stay away from change. It's an avalanche—
all the rocks sliding down the mountain, and the child standing underneath
just gets killed.

They sit in the best place, under the poplars.
And they talk—it must be hours now, the sun's in a different place.
About school, about people they both know,
about being adult, about how you knew what your dreams were.

They used to play games, but that's stopped now—too much touching.
They only touch each other when they fold the blanket.

They know this in each other.
That's why it isn't talked about.
Before they do anything like that, they'll need to know more—
in fact, everything that can happen. Until then, they'll just watch
and stay children.

Today she's folding the blanket alone, to be safe.
And he looks away—he pretends to be too lost in thought to help out.

They know that at some point you stop being children, and at that point
you become strangers. It seems unbearably lonely.

When they get home to the village, it's nearly twilight.
It's been a perfect day; they talk about this,
about when they'll have a chance to have a picnic again.

They walk through the summer dusk,
not holding hands but still telling each other everything.

Rain tomorrow, but tonight the sky is clear, the stars shine.
Still, the rain's coming,
maybe enough to drown the seeds.
There's a wind from the sea pushing the clouds;
before you see them, you feel the wind.
Better look at the fields now,
see how they look before they're flooded.

A full moon. Yesterday, a sheep escaped into the woods,
and not just any sheep—the ram, the whole future.
If we see him again, we'll see his bones.

The grass shudders a little; maybe the wind passed through it.
And the new leaves of the olives shudder in the same way.
Mice in the fields. Where the fox hunts,
tomorrow there'll be blood in the grass.
But the storm—the storm will wash it away.

In one window, there's a boy sitting.
He's been sent to bed—too early,
in his opinion. So he sits at the window—

Everything is settled now.
Where you are now is where you'll sleep, where you'll wake up in the
    morning.
The mountain stands like a beacon, to remind the night that the earth exists,
that it mustn't be forgotten.

Above the sea, the clouds form as the wind rises,
dispersing them, giving them a sense of purpose.

Tomorrow the dawn won't come.
The sky won't go back to being the sky of day; it will go on as night,
except the stars will fade and vanish as the storm arrives,
lasting perhaps ten hours altogether.
But the world as it was cannot return.

One by one, the lights of the village houses dim
and the mountain shines in the darkness with reflected light.

No sound. Only cats scuffling in the doorways.
They smell the wind: time to make more cats.
Later, they prowl the streets, but the smell of the wind stalks them.
It's the same in the fields, confused by the smell of blood,
though for now only the wind rises; stars turn the field silver.

This far from the sea and still we know these signs.
The night is an open book.
But the world beyond the night remains a mystery.

SUNSET

At the same time as the sun's setting,
a farm worker's burning dead leaves.

It's nothing, this fire.
It's a small thing, controlled,
like a family run by a dictator.

Still, when it blazes up, the farm worker disappears;
from the road, he's invisible.

Compared to the sun, all the fires here
are short-lived, amateurish—
they end when the leaves are gone.
Then the farm worker reappears, raking the ashes.

But the death is real.
As though the sun's done what it came to do,
made the field grow, then
inspired the burning of earth.

So it can set now.

IN THE CAFÉ

It's natural to be tired of earth.
When you've been dead this long, you'll probably be tired of heaven.
You do what you can do in a place
but after a while you exhaust that place,
so you long for rescue.

My friend falls in love a little too easily.
Every year or so a new girl—
If they have children he doesn't mind;
he can fall in love with children also.

So the rest of us get sour and he stays the same,
full of adventure, always making new discoveries.
But he hates moving, so the women have to come from here, or near here.

Every month or so, we meet for coffee.
In summer, we'll walk around the meadow, sometimes as far as the mountain.
Even when he suffers, he's thriving, happy in his body.
It's partly the women, of course, but not that only.

He moves into their houses, learns to like the movies they like.
It's not an act—he really does learn,
the way someone goes to cooking school and learns to cook.

He sees everything with their eyes.
He becomes not what they are but what they could be
if they weren't trapped in their characters.
For him, this new self of his is liberating because it's invented—

he absorbs the fundamental needs in which their souls are rooted,
he experiences as his own the rituals and preferences these give rise to—
but as he lives with each woman, he inhabits each version of himself
fully, because it isn't compromised by the normal shame and anxiety.

When he leaves, the women are devastated.
Finally they met a man who answered all their needs—
there was nothing they couldn't tell him.
When they meet him now, he's a cipher—
the person they knew doesn't exist anymore.
He came into existence when they met,
he vanished when it ended, when he walked away.

After a few years, they get over him.
They tell their new boyfriends how amazing it was,
like living with another woman, but without the spite, the envy,
and with a man's strength, a man's clarity of mind.

And the men tolerate this, they even smile.
They stroke the women's hair—
they know this man doesn't exist; it's hard for them to feel competitive.

You couldn't ask, though, for a better friend,
a more subtle observer. When we talk, he's candid and open,
he's kept the intensity we all had when we were young.
He talks openly of fear, of the qualities he detests in himself.
And he's generous—he knows how I am just by looking.
If I'm frustrated or angry, he'll listen for hours,
not because he's forcing himself, because he's interested.

I guess that's how he is with the women.
But the friends he never leaves—
with them, he's trying to stand outside his life, to see it clearly—

Today he wants to sit; there's a lot to say,
too much for the meadow. He wants to be face to face,
talking to someone he's known forever.

He's on the verge of a new life.
His eyes glow, he isn't interested in the coffee.
Even though it's sunset, for him
the sun is rising again, and the fields are flushed with dawn light,
rose-colored and tentative.

He's himself in these moments, not pieces of the women
he's slept with. He enters their lives as you enter a dream,
without volition, and he lives there as you live in a dream,
however long it lasts. And in the morning, you remember
nothing of the dream at all, nothing at all.

For two weeks he's been watching the same girl,
someone he sees in the plaza. In her twenties maybe,
drinking coffee in the afternoon, the little dark head
bent over a magazine.
He watches from across the square, pretending
to be buying something, cigarettes, maybe a bouquet of flowers.

Because she doesn't know it exists,
her power is very great now, fused to the needs of his imagination.
He is her prisoner. She says the words he gives her
in a voice he imagines, low-pitched and soft,
a voice from the south as the dark hair must be from the south.

Soon she will recognize him, then begin to expect him.
And perhaps then every day her hair will be freshly washed,
she will gaze outward across the plaza before looking down.
And after that they will become lovers.

But he hopes this will not happen immediately
since whatever power she exerts now over his body, over his emotions,
she will have no power once she commits herself—

she will withdraw into that private world of feeling
women enter when they love. And living there, she will become
like a person who casts no shadow, who is not present in the world;
in that sense, so little use to him
it hardly matters whether she lives or dies.

DAWN

1.

Child waking up in a dark room
screaming I want my duck back, I want my duck back

in a language nobody understands in the least—

There is no duck.

But the dog, all upholstered in white plush—
the dog is right there in the crib next to him.

Years and years—that's how much time passes.
All in a dream. But the duck—
no one knows what happened to that.

2.

They've just met, now
they're sleeping near an open window.

Partly to wake them, to assure them
that what they remember of the night is correct,
now light needs to enter the room,

also to show them the context in which this occurred:
socks half hidden under a dirty mat,
quilt decorated with green leaves—

the sunlight specifying
these but not other objects,
setting boundaries, sure of itself, not arbitrary,

then lingering, describing
each thing in detail,
fastidious, like a composition in English,
even a little blood on the sheets—

3.

Afterward, they separate for the day.
Even later, at a desk, in the market,
the manager not satisfied with the figures he's given,
the berries moldy under the topmost layer—

so that one withdraws from the world
even as one continues to take action in it—

You get home, that's when you notice the mold.
Too late, in other words.

As though the sun blinded you for a moment.

FIRST SNOW

Like a child, the earth's going to sleep,
or so the story goes.

But I'm not tired, it says.
And the mother says, You may not be tired but I'm tired—

You can see it in her face, everyone can.
So the snow has to fall, sleep has to come.
Because the mother's sick to death of her life
and needs silence.

EARTHWORM

Mortal standing on top of the earth, refusing
to enter the earth: you tell yourself
you are able to see deeply
the conflicts of which you are made but, facing death,
you will not dig deeply—if you sense
that pity engulfs you, you are not
delusional: not all pity
descends from higher to lesser, some
arises out of the earth itself, persistent
yet devoid of coercion. We can be split in two, but you are
mutilated at the core, your mind
detached from your feelings—
repression does not deceive
organisms like ourselves:
once you enter the earth, you will not fear the earth;
once you inhabit your terror,
death will come to seem a web of channels or tunnels like
a sponge's or honeycomb's, which, as part of us,
you will be free to explore. Perhaps
you will find in these travels
a wholeness that eluded you—as men and women
you were never free
to register in your body whatever left
a mark on your spirit.

AT THE RIVER

One night that summer my mother decided it was time to tell me about
what she referred to as *pleasure*, though you could see she felt
some sort of unease about this ceremony, which she tried to cover up
by first taking my hand, as though somebody in the family had just died—
she went on holding my hand as she made her speech,
which was more like a speech about mechanical engineering
than a conversation about pleasure. In her other hand,
she had a book from which, apparently, she'd taken the main facts.
She did the same thing with the others, my two brothers and sister,
and the book was always the same book, dark blue,
though we each got our own copy.

There was a line drawing on the cover
showing a man and woman holding hands
but standing fairly far apart, like people on two sides of a dirt road.

Obviously, she and my father did not have a language for what they did
which, from what I could judge, wasn't pleasure.
At the same time, whatever holds human beings together
could hardly resemble those cool black-and-white diagrams, which suggested,
among other things, that you could only achieve pleasure
with a person of the opposite sex,
so you didn't get two sockets, say, and no plug.

School wasn't in session.
I went back to my room and shut the door
and my mother went into the kitchen
where my father was pouring glasses of wine for himself and his invisible guest
who—surprise—doesn't appear.
No, it's just my father and his friend the Holy Ghost
partying the night away until the bottle runs out,
after which my father continues sitting at the table
with an open book in front of him.

Tactfully, so as not to embarrass the Spirit,
my father handled all the glasses,
first his own, then the other, back and forth like every other night.

By then, I was out of the house.
It was summer; my friends used to meet at the river.
The whole thing seemed a grave embarrassment
although the truth was that, except for the boys, maybe we didn't
    understand mechanics.
The boys had the key right in front of them, in their hands if they wanted,
and many of them said they'd already used it,
though once one boy said this, the others said it too,
and of course people had older brothers and sisters.

We sat at the edge of the river discussing parents in general
and sex in particular. And a lot of information got shared,
and of course the subject was unfailingly interesting.
I showed people my book, *Ideal Marriage*—we all had a good laugh over it.
One night a boy brought a bottle of wine and we passed it around for a while.

More and more that summer we understood
that something was going to happen to us
that would change us.
And the group, all of us who used to meet this way,
the group would shatter, like a shell that falls away
so the bird can emerge.
Only of course it would be two birds emerging, pairs of birds.

We sat in the reeds at the edge of the river
throwing small stones. When the stones hit,
you could see the stars multiply for a second, little explosions of light
flashing and going out. There was a boy I was beginning to like,
not to speak to but to watch.
I liked to sit behind him to study the back of his neck.

And after a while we'd all get up together and walk back through the dark
to the village. Above the field, the sky was clear,
stars everywhere, like in the river, though these were the real stars,
even the dead ones were real.

But the ones in the river—
they were like having some idea that explodes suddenly into a thousand ideas,
not real, maybe, but somehow more lifelike.

When I got home, my mother was asleep, my father was still at the table,
reading his book. And I said, Did your friend go away?
And he looked at me intently for a while,
then he said, Your mother and I used to drink a glass of wine together
after dinner.

There's an open door through which you can see the kitchen—
always some wonderful smell coming from there,
but what paralyzes him is the warmth of that place,
the stove in the center giving out heat—

Some lives are like that.
Heat's at the center, so constant no one gives it a thought.
But the key he's holding unlocks a different door,
and on the other side, warmth isn't waiting for him.
He makes it himself—him and the wine.

The first glass is himself coming home.
He can smell the daube, a smell of red wine and orange peel mixed in
    with the veal.
His wife is singing in the bedroom, putting the children to sleep.
He drinks slowly, letting his wife open the door, her finger to her lips,
and then letting her eagerly rush toward him to embrace him.
And afterward there will be the daube.

But the glasses that follow cause her to disappear.
She takes the children with her; the apartment shrinks back to what it was.
He has found someone else—not another person exactly,
but a self who despises intimacy, as though the privacy of marriage
is a door that two people shut together
and no one can get out alone, not the wife, not the husband,
so the heat gets trapped there until they suffocate,
as though they were living in a phone booth—

Then the wine is gone. He washes his face, wanders around the apartment.
It's summer—life rots in the heat.
Some nights, he still hears a woman singing to her children;
other nights, behind the bedroom door, her naked body doesn't exist.

FATIGUE

All winter he sleeps.
Then he gets up, he shaves—
it takes a long time to become a man again,
his face in the mirror bristles with dark hair.

The earth now is like a woman, waiting for him.
A great hopefulness—that's what binds them together,
himself and this woman.

Now he has to work all day to prove he deserves what he has.
Midday: he's tired, he's thirsty.
But if he quits now he'll have nothing.

The sweat covering his back and arms
is like his life pouring out of him
with nothing replacing it.

He works like an animal, then
like a machine, with no feeling.
But the bond will never break
though the earth fights back now, wild in the summer heat—

He squats down, letting the dirt run through his fingers.

The sun goes down, the dark comes.
Now that summer's over, the earth is hard, cold;
by the road, a few isolated fires burn.

Nothing remains of love,
only estrangement and hatred.

Not far from the house and barn,
the farm worker's burning dead leaves.

They don't disappear voluntarily;
you have to prod them along
as the farm worker prods the leaf pile every year
until it releases a smell of smoke into the air.

And then, for an hour or so, it's really animated,
blazing away like something alive.

When the smoke clears, the house is safe.
A woman's standing in the back,
folding dry clothes into a willow basket.

So it's finished for another year,
death making room for life,
as much as possible,
but burning the house would be too much room.

Sunset. Across the road,
the farm worker's sweeping the cold ashes.
Sometimes a few escape, harmlessly drifting around in the wind.

Then the air is still.
Where the fire was, there's only bare dirt in a circle of rocks.
Nothing between the earth and the dark.

WALKING AT NIGHT

Now that she is old,
the young men don't approach her
so the nights are free,
the streets at dusk that were so dangerous
have become as safe as the meadow.

By midnight, the town's quiet.
Moonlight reflects off the stone walls;
on the pavement, you can hear the nervous sounds
of the men rushing home to their wives and mothers; this late,
the doors are locked, the windows darkened.

When they pass, they don't notice her.
She's like a dry blade of grass in a field of grasses.
So her eyes that used never to leave the ground
are free now to go where they like.

When she's tired of the streets, in good weather she walks
in the fields where the town ends.
Sometimes, in summer, she goes as far as the river.

The young people used to gather not far from here
but now the river's grown shallow from lack of rain, so
the bank's deserted—

There were picnics then.
The boys and girls eventually paired off;
after a while, they made their way into the woods
where it's always twilight—

The woods would be empty now—
the naked bodies have found other places to hide.

In the river, there's just enough water for the night sky
to make patterns against the gray stones. The moon's bright,
one stone among many others. And the wind rises;
it blows the small trees that grow at the river's edge.

When you look at a body you see a history.
Once that body isn't seen anymore,
the story it tried to tell gets lost—

On nights like this, she'll walk as far as the bridge
before she turns back.
Everything still smells of summer.
And her body begins to seem again the body she had as a young woman,
glistening under the light summer clothing.

On most days, the sun wakes me.
Even on dark days, there's a lot of light in the mornings—
thin lines where the blinds don't come together.
It's morning—I open my eyes.
And every morning I see again how dirty this place is, how grim.
So I'm never late for work—this isn't a place to spend time in,
watching the dirt pile up as the sun brightens.

During the day at work, I forget about it.
I think about work: getting colored beads into plastic vials.
When I get home at dusk, the room is shadowy—
the shadow of the bureau covers the bare floor.
It's telling me whoever lives here is doomed.

When I'm in moods like that,
I go to a bar, watch sports on television.

Sometimes I talk to the owner.
He says moods don't mean anything—
the shadows mean night is coming, not that daylight will never return.
He tells me to move the bureau; I'll get different shadows, maybe
a different diagnosis.

If we're alone, he turns down the volume of the television.
The players keep crashing into each other
but all we hear are our own voices.

If there's no game, he'll pick a film.
It's the same thing—the sound stays off, so there's only images.
When the film's over, we compare notes, to see if we both saw the same story.
Sometimes we spend hours watching this junk.

When I walk home it's night. You can't see for once how shabby the houses are.
The film is in my head: I tell myself I'm following the path of the hero.

The hero ventures out—that's dawn.
When he's gone, the camera collects pictures of other things.
When he gets back, it already knows everything there is to know,
just from watching the room.

There's no shadows now.
Inside the room, it's dark; the night air is cool.
In summer, you can smell the orange blossoms.
If there's wind, one tree will do it—you don't need the whole orchard.

I do what the hero does.
He opens the window. He has his reunion with earth.

HUNTERS

A dark night—the streets belong to the cats.
The cats and whatever small thing they find to kill—
The cats are fast like their ancestors in the hills
and hungry like their ancestors.

Hardly any moon. So the night's cool—
no moon to heat it up. Summer's on the way out
but for now there's still plenty to hunt
though the mice are quiet, watchful like the cats.

Smell the air—a still night, a night for love.
And every once in a while a scream
rising from the street below
where the cat's digging his teeth into the rat's leg.

Once the rat screams, it's dead. That scream is like a map:
it tells the cat where to find the throat. After that,
the scream's coming from a corpse.

You're lucky to be in love on nights like this,
still warm enough to lie naked on top of the sheets,
sweating, because it's hard work, this love, no matter what anyone says.

The dead rats lie in the street, where the cat drops them.
Be glad you're not on the street now,
before the street cleaners come to sweep them away. When the sun rises,
it won't be disappointed with the world it finds,
the streets will be clean for the new day and the night that follows.

Just be glad you were in bed,
where the cries of love drown out the screams of the corpses.

Today I went to the doctor—
the doctor said I was dying,
not in those words, but when I said it
she didn't deny it—

What have you done to your body, her silence says.
We gave it to you and look what you did to it,
how you abused it.
I'm not talking only of cigarettes, she says,
but also of poor diet, of drink.

She's a young woman; the stiff white coat disguises her body.
Her hair's pulled back, the little female wisps
suppressed by a dark band. She's not at ease here,

behind her desk, with her diploma over her head,
reading a list of numbers in columns,
some flagged for her attention.
Her spine's straight also, showing no feeling.

No one taught me how to care for my body.
You grow up watched by your mother or grandmother.
Once you're free of them, your wife takes over, but she's nervous,
she doesn't go too far. So this body I have,
that the doctor blames me for—it's always been supervised by women,
and let me tell you, they left a lot out.

The doctor looks at me—
between us, a stack of books and folders.
Except for us, the clinic's empty.

There's a trap-door here, and through that door,
the country of the dead. And the living push you through,
they want you there first, ahead of them.

The doctor knows this. She has her books,
I have my cigarettes. Finally
she writes something on a slip of paper.
This will help your blood pressure, she says.

And I pocket it, a sign to go.
And once I'm outside, I tear it up, like a ticket to the other world.

She was crazy to come here,
a place where she knows no one.
She's alone; she has no wedding ring.
She goes home alone, to her place outside the village.
And she has her one glass of wine a day,
her dinner that isn't a dinner.

And she takes off that white coat:
between that coat and her body,
there's just a thin layer of cotton.
And at some point, that comes off too.

To get born, your body makes a pact with death,
and from that moment, all it tries to do is cheat—

You get into bed alone. Maybe you sleep, maybe you never wake up.
But for a long time you hear every sound.
It's a night like any summer night; the dark never comes.

BATS

There are two kinds of vision:
the seeing of things, which belongs
to the science of optics, versus
the seeing beyond things, which
results from deprivation. Man mocking the dark, rejecting
worlds you do not know: though the dark
is full of obstacles, it is possible to have
intense awareness when the field is narrow
and the signals few. Night has bred in us
thought more focused than yours, if rudimentary:
man the ego, man imprisoned in the eye,
there is a path you cannot see, beyond the eye's reach,
what the philosophers have called
the *via negativa*: to make a place for light
the mystic shuts his eyes—illumination
of the kind he seeks destroys
creatures who depend on things.

BURNING LEAVES

The fire burns up into the clear sky,
eager and furious, like an animal trying to get free,
to run wild as nature intended—

When it burns like this,
leaves aren't enough—it's
acquisitive, rapacious,

refusing to be contained, to accept limits—

There's a pile of stones around it.
Past the stones, the earth's raked clean, bare—

Finally the leaves are gone, the fuel's gone,
the last flames burn upwards and sidewards—

Concentric rings of stones and gray earth
circle a few sparks;
the farmer stomps on these with his boots.

It's impossible to believe this will work—
not with a fire like this, those last sparks
still resisting, unfinished,
believing they will get everything in the end

since it is obvious they are not defeated,
merely dormant or resting, though no one knows
whether they represent life or death.

MARCH

The light stays longer in the sky, but it's a cold light,
it brings no relief from winter.

My neighbor stares out the window,
talking to her dog. He's sniffing the garden,
trying to reach a decision about the dead flowers.

It's a little early for all this.
Everything's still very bare—
nevertheless, something's different today from yesterday.

We can see the mountain: the peak's glittering where the ice catches the light.
But on the sides the snow's melted, exposing bare rock.

My neighbor's calling the dog, making her unconvincing doglike sounds.
The dog's polite; he raises his head when she calls,
but he doesn't move. So she goes on calling,
her failed bark slowly deteriorating into a human voice.

All her life she dreamed of living by the sea
but fate didn't put her there.
It laughed at her dreams;
it locked her up in the hills, where no one escapes.

The sun beats down on the earth, the earth flourishes.
And every winter, it's as though the rock underneath the earth rises
higher and higher and the earth becomes rock, cold and rejecting.

She says hope killed her parents, it killed her grandparents.
It rose up each spring with the wheat
and died between the heat of summer and the raw cold.
In the end, they told her to live near the sea,
as though that would make a difference.

By late spring she'll be garrulous, but now she's down to two words,
never and *only*, to express this sense that life's cheated her.

Never the cries of the gulls, only, in summer, the crickets, cicadas.
Only the smell of the field, when all she wanted
was the smell of the sea, of disappearance.

The sky above the fields has turned a sort of grayish pink
as the sun sinks. The clouds are silk yarn, magenta and crimson.

And everywhere the earth is rustling, not lying still.
And the dog senses this stirring; his ears twitch.

He walks back and forth, vaguely remembering
from other years this elation. The season of discoveries
is beginning. Always the same discoveries, but to the dog,
intoxicating and new, not duplicitous.

I tell my neighbor we'll be like this
when we lose our memories. I ask her if she's ever seen the sea
and she says, once, in a movie.
It was a sad story, nothing worked out at all.

The lovers part. The sea hammers the shore, the mark each wave leaves
wiped out by the wave that follows.
Never accumulation, never one wave trying to build on another,
never the promise of shelter—

The sea doesn't change as the earth changes;
it doesn't lie.
You ask the sea, what can you promise me
and it speaks the truth; it says *erasure*.

Finally the dog goes in.
We watch the crescent moon,
very faint at first, then clearer and clearer
as the night grows dark.
Soon it will be the sky of early spring, stretching above the stubborn ferns
and violets.

Nothing can be forced to live.
The earth is like a drug now, like a voice from far away,
a lover or master. In the end, you do what the voice tells you.
It says forget, you forget.
It says begin again, you begin again.

A NIGHT IN SPRING

They told her she came out of a hole in her mother
but really it's impossible to believe
something so delicate could come out of something
so fat—her mother naked
looks like a pig. She wants to think
the children telling her were making fun of her ignorance;
they think they can tell her anything
because she doesn't come from the country, where people know these things.

She wants the subject to be finished, dead. It troubles her
to picture this space in her mother's body,
releasing human beings now and again,
first hiding them, then dropping them into the world,

and all along drugging them, inspiring the same feelings
she attaches to her bed, this sense of solitude, this calm,
this sense of being unique—

Maybe her mother still has these feelings.
This could explain why she never sees
the great differences between the two of them

because at one point they *were* the same person—

She sees her face in the mirror, the small nose
sunk in fat, and at the same time she hears
the children's laughter as they tell her
it doesn't start in the face, stupid,
it starts in the body—

At night in bed, she pulls the quilt as high as possible,
up to her neck—

She has found this thing, a self,
and come to cherish it,
and now it will be packed away in flesh and lost—

And she feels her mother did this to her, meant this to happen.
Because whatever she may try to do with her mind,
her body will disobey,
that its complacency, its finality, will make her mind invisible,
no one will see—

Very gently, she moves the sheet aside.
And under it, there is her body, still beautiful and new
with no marks anywhere. And it seems to her still
identical to her mind, so consistent with it as to seem
transparent, almost,

and once again
she falls in love with it and vows to protect it.

HARVEST

It's autumn in the market—
not wise anymore to buy tomatoes.
They're beautiful still on the outside,
some perfectly round and red, the rare varieties
misshapen, individual, like human brains covered in red oilcloth—

Inside, they're gone. Black, moldy—
you can't take a bite without anxiety.
Here and there, among the tainted ones, a fruit
still perfect, picked before decay set in.

Instead of tomatoes, crops nobody really wants.
Pumpkins, a lot of pumpkins.
Gourds, ropes of dried chilies, braids of garlic.
The artisans weave dead flowers into wreaths;
they tie bits of colored yarn around dried lavender.
And people go on for a while buying these things
as though they thought the farmers would see to it
that things went back to normal:
the vines would go back to bearing new peas;
the first small lettuces, so fragile, so delicate, would begin
to poke out of the dirt.

Instead, it gets dark early.
And the rains get heavier; they carry
the weight of dead leaves.

At dusk, now, an atmosphere of threat, of foreboding.
And people feel this themselves; they give a name to the season,
harvest, to put a better face on these things.

The gourds are rotting on the ground, the sweet blue grapes are finished.
A few roots, maybe, but the ground's so hard the farmers think
it isn't worth the effort to dig them out. For what?
To stand in the marketplace under a thin umbrella, in the rain, in the cold,
no customers anymore?

And then the frost comes; there's no more question of harvest.
The snow begins; the pretense of life ends.
The earth is white now; the fields shine when the moon rises.

I sit at the bedroom window, watching the snow fall.
The earth is like a mirror:
calm meeting calm, detachment meeting detachment.

What lives, lives underground.
What dies, dies without struggle.

CONFESSION

He steals sometimes, because they don't have their own tree
and he loves fruit. Not steals exactly—
he pretends he's an animal; he eats off the ground,
as the animals would eat. This is what he tells the priest,
that he doesn't think it should be a sin to take what would just lie there
    and rot,
this year like every other year.

As a man, as a human being, the priest agrees with the boy,
but as a priest he chastises him, though the penance is light,
so as to not kill off imagination: what he'd give
to a much younger boy who took something that wasn't his.

But the boy objects. He's willing to do the penance
because he likes the priest, but he refuses to believe that Jesus
gave this fig tree to this woman; he wants to know
what Jesus does with all the money he gets from real estate,
not just in this village but in the whole country.

Partly he's joking but partly he's serious
and the priest gets irritated—he's out of his depth with this boy,
he can't explain that though Christ doesn't deal in property,
still the fig tree belongs to the woman, even if she never picks the figs.
Perhaps one day, with the boy's encouragement,
the woman will become a saint and share her fig tree and her big house
    with strangers,
but for the moment she's a human being whose ancestors built this house.

The priest is pleased to have moved the conversation away from money,
which makes him nervous, and back to words like *family* or *tradition*,
where he feels more secure. The boy stares at him—

he knows perfectly well the ways in which he's taken advantage of a senile
    old lady,
the ways he's tried to charm the priest, to impress him. But he despises
speeches like the one beginning now;
he wants to taunt the priest with his own flight: if he loves family so much,
why didn't the priest marry as his parents married, continue the line from
    which he came.

But he's silent. The words that mean there will be
no questioning, no trying to reason—those words have been uttered.
"Thank you, Father," he says.

MARRIAGE

All week they've been by the sea again
and the sound of the sea colors everything.
Blue sky fills the window.
But the only sound is the sound of the waves pounding the shore—
angry. Angry at something. Whatever it is
must be why he's turned away. Angry, though he'd never hit her,
never say a word, probably.

So it's up to her to get the answer some other way,
from the sea, maybe, or the gray clouds suddenly
rising above it. The smell of the sea is in the sheets,
the smell of sun and wind, the hotel smell, fresh and sweet
because they're changed every day.

He never uses words. Words, for him, are for making arrangements,
for doing business. Never for anger, never for tenderness.

She strokes his back. She puts her face up against it,
even though it's like putting your face against a wall.

And the silence between them is ancient: it says
these are the boundaries.

He isn't sleeping, not even pretending to sleep.
His breathing's not regular: he breathes in with reluctance;
he doesn't want to commit himself to being alive.
And he breathes out fast, like a king banishing a servant.

Beneath the silence, the sound of the sea,
the sea's violence spreading everywhere, not finished, not finished,
his breath driving the waves—

But she knows who she is and she knows what she wants.
As long as that's true, something so natural can't hurt her.

Spring comes quickly: overnight
the plum tree blossoms,
the warm air fills with bird calls.

In the plowed dirt, someone has drawn a picture of the sun
with rays coming out all around
but because the background is dirt, the sun is black.
There is no signature.

Alas, very soon everything will disappear:
the bird calls, the delicate blossoms. In the end,
even the earth itself will follow the artist's name into oblivion.

Nevertheless, the artist intends
a mood of celebration.

How beautiful the blossoms are—emblems of the resilience of life.
The birds approach eagerly.

FIGS

My mother made figs in wine—
poached with cloves, sometimes a few peppercorns.
Black figs, from our tree.
And the wine was red, the pepper left a taste of smoke in the syrup.
I used to feel I was in another country.

Before that, there'd be chicken.
In autumn, sometimes filled with wild mushrooms.
There wasn't always time for that.
And the weather had to be right, just after the rain.
Sometimes it was just chicken, with a lemon inside.

She'd open the wine. Nothing special—
something she got from the neighbors.
I miss that wine—what I buy now doesn't taste as good.

I make these things for my husband,
but he doesn't like them.
He wants his mother's dishes, but I don't make them well.
When I try, I get angry—

He's trying to turn me into a person I never was.
He thinks it's a simple thing—
you cut up a chicken, throw a few tomatoes into the pan.
Garlic, if there's garlic.
An hour later, you're in paradise.

He thinks it's my job to learn, not his job
to teach me. What my mother cooked, I don't need to learn.
My hands already knew, just from smelling the cloves
while I did my homework.
When it was my turn, I was right. I did know.
The first time I tasted them, my childhood came back.

When we were young, it was different.
My husband and I—we were in love. All we ever wanted
was to touch each other.

He comes home, he's tired.
Everything is hard—making money is hard, watching your body change
is hard. You can take these problems when you're young—
something's difficult for a while, but you're confident.
If it doesn't work out, you'll do something else.

He minds summer most—the sun gets to him.
Here it's merciless, you can feel the world aging.
The grass turns dry, the gardens get full of weeds and slugs.

It was the best time for us once.
The hours of light when he came home from work—
we'd turn them into hours of darkness.
Everything was a big secret—
even the things we said every night.

And slowly the sun would go down;
we'd see the lights of the city come on.
The nights were glossy with stars—stars
glittered above the high buildings.

Sometimes we'd light a candle.
But most nights, no. Most nights we'd lie there in the darkness,
with our arms around each other.

But there was a sense you could control the light—
it was a wonderful feeling; you could make the whole room
bright again, or you could lie in the night air,
listening to the cars.

We'd get quiet after a while. The night would get quiet.
But we didn't sleep, we didn't want to give up consciousness.
We had given the night permission to carry us along;
we lay there, not interfering. Hour after hour, each one
listening to the other's breath, watching the light change
in the window at the end of the bed—

whatever happened in that window,
we were in harmony with it.

AT THE DANCE

Twice a year we hung the Christmas lights—
at Christmas for our Lord's birth, and at the end of August,
as a blessing on the harvest—
near the end but before the end,
and everyone would come to see,
even the oldest people who could hardly walk—

They had to see the colored lights,
and in summer there was always music, too—
music and dancing.

For the young, it was everything.
Your life was made here—what was finished under the stars
started in the lights of the plaza.
Haze of cigarettes, the women gathered under the colored awnings
singing along with whatever songs were popular that year,
cheeks brown from the sun and red from the wine.

I remember all of it—my friends and I, how we were changed by the music,
and the women, I remember how bold they were, the timid ones
along with the others—

A spell was on us, but it was a sickness too,
the men and women choosing each other almost by accident, randomly,
and the lights glittering, misleading,
because whatever you did then you did forever—

And it seemed at the time
such a game, really—lighthearted, casual,
dissipating like smoke, like perfume between a woman's breasts,
intense because your eyes are closed.

How were these things decided?
By smell, by feel—a man would approach a woman,
ask her to dance, but what it meant was
will you let me touch you, and the woman could say
many things, ask me later, she could say, ask me again.
Or she could say no, and turn away,
as though if nothing but you happened that night
you still weren't enough, or she could say yes, I'd love to dance
which meant yes, I want to be touched.

SOLITUDE

It's very dark today; through the rain,
the mountain isn't visible. The only sound
is rain, driving life underground.
And with the rain, cold comes.
There will be no moon tonight, no stars.

The wind rose at night;
all morning it lashed against the wheat—
at noon it ended. But the storm went on,
soaking the dry fields, then flooding them—

The earth has vanished.
There's nothing to see, only the rain
gleaming against the dark windows.
This is the resting place, where nothing moves—

Now we return to what we were,
animals living in darkness
without language or vision—

Nothing proves I'm alive.
There is only the rain, the rain is endless.

EARTHWORM

It is not sad not to be human
nor is living entirely within the earth
demeaning or empty: it is the nature of the mind
to defend its eminence, as it is the nature of those
who walk on the surface to fear the depths—one's
position determines one's feelings. And yet
to walk on top of a thing is not to prevail over it—
it is more the opposite, a disguised dependency,
by which the slave completes the master. Likewise
the mind disdains what it can't control,
which will in turn destroy it. It is not painful to return
without language or vision: if, like the Buddhists,
one declines to leave
inventories of the self, one emerges in a space
the mind cannot conceive, being wholly physical, not
metaphoric. What is your word? *Infinity*, meaning
that which cannot be measured.

The building's brick, so the walls get warm in summer.
When the summer goes, they're still warm,
especially on the south side—you feel the sun there, in the brick,
as though it meant to leave its stamp on the wall, not just sail over it
on its way to the hills. I take my breaks here, leaning against the wall,
smoking cigarettes.

The bosses don't mind—they joke that if the business fails,
they'll just rent wall space. Big joke—everyone laughs very loud.
But you can't eat—they don't want rats here, looking for scraps.

Some of the others don't care about being warm, feeling the sun on their
    backs
from the warm brick. They want to know where the views are.
To me, it isn't important what I see. I grew up in those hills;
I'll be buried there. In between, I don't need to keep sneaking looks.

My wife says when I say things like this my mouth goes bitter.
She loves the village—every day she misses her mother.
She misses her youth—how we met there and fell in love.
How our children were born there. She knows she'll never go back
but she keeps hoping—

At night in bed, her eyes film over. She talks about the olive trees,
the long silver leaves shimmering in the sunlight.
And the bark, the trees themselves, so supple, pale gray like the rocks
    behind them.

She remembers picking the olives, who made the best brine.
I remember her hands then, smelling of vinegar.
And the bitter taste of the olives, before you knew not to eat them
fresh off the tree.

And I remind her how useless they were without people to cure them.
Brine them, set them out in the sun—
And I tell her all nature is like that to me, useless and bitter.
It's like a trap—and you fall into it because of the olive leaves,
because they're beautiful.

You grow up looking at the hills, how the sun sets behind them.
And the olive trees, waving and shimmering. And you realize that if you don't
    get out fast
you'll die, as though this beauty were gagging you so you couldn't breathe—

And I tell her I know we're trapped here. But better to be trapped
by decent men, who even re-do the lunchroom,
than by the sun and the hills. When I complain here,
my voice is heard—somebody's voice is heard. There's dispute, there's anger.
But human beings are talking to each other, the way my wife and I talk.
Talking even when they don't agree, when one of them is only pretending.

In the other life, your despair just turns into silence.
The sun disappears behind the western hills—
when it comes back, there's no reference at all to your suffering.
So your voice dies away. You stop trying, not just with the sun,
but with human beings. And the small things that made you happy
can't get through to you anymore.

I know things are hard here. And the owners—I know they lie sometimes.
But there are truths that ruin a life; the same way, some lies
are generous, warm and cozy like the sun on the brick wall.

So when you think of the wall, you don't think *prison*.
More the opposite—you think of everything you escaped, being here.

And then my wife gives up for the night, she turns her back.
Some nights she cries a little.
Her only weapon was the truth—it is true, the hills are beautiful.
And the olive trees really are like silver.

But a person who accepts a lie, who accepts support from it
because it's warm, it's pleasant for a little while—
that person she'll never understand, no matter how much she loves him.

SUNRISE

This time of year, the window boxes smell of the hills,
the thyme and rosemary that grew there,
crammed into the narrow spaces between the rocks
and, lower down, where there was real dirt,
competing with other things, blueberries and currants,
the small shrubby trees the bees love—
Whatever we ate smelled of the hills,
even when there was almost nothing.
Or maybe that's what nothing tastes like, thyme and rosemary.

Maybe, too, that's what it looks like—
beautiful, like the hills, the rocks above the tree line
webbed with sweet-smelling herbs,
the small plants glittering with dew—

It was a big event to climb up there and wait for dawn,
seeing what the sun sees as it slides out from behind the rocks,
and what you couldn't see, you imagined;

your eyes would go as far as they could, to the river, say,
and your mind would do the rest—

And if you missed a day, there was always the next,
and if you missed a year, it didn't matter,
the hills weren't going anywhere,
the thyme and rosemary kept coming back,
the sun kept rising, the bushes kept bearing fruit—

The streetlight's off: that's dawn here.
It's on: that's twilight.
Either way, no one looks up. Everyone just pushes ahead,
and the smell of the past is everywhere,
the thyme and rosemary rubbing against your clothes,
the smell of too many illusions—

I went back but I didn't stay.
Everyone I cared about was gone,
some dead, some disappeared into one of those places that don't exist,
the ones we dreamed about because we saw them from the top of the hills—
I had to see if the fields were still shining,
the sun telling the same lies about how beautiful the world is
when all you need to know of a place is, do people live there.
If they do, you know everything.

Between them, the hills and sky took up all the room.
Whatever was left, that was ours for a while.
But sooner or later the hills will take it back, give it to the animals.
And maybe the moon will send the seas there
and where we once lived will be a stream or river coiling around the base of
    the hills,
paying the sky the compliment of reflection—

Blue in summer. White when the snow falls.

A WARM DAY

Today the sun was shining
so my neighbor washed her nightdresses in the river—
she comes home with everything folded in a basket,
beaming, as though her life had just been
lengthened a decade. Cleanliness makes her happy—
it says you can begin again,
the old mistakes needn't hold you back.

A good neighbor—we leave each other
to our privacies. Just now,
she's singing to herself, pinning the damp wash to the line.

Little by little, days like this
will seem normal. But winter was hard:
the nights coming early, the dawns dark
with a gray, persistent rain—months of that,
and then the snow, like silence coming from the sky,
obliterating the trees and gardens.

Today, all that's past us.
The birds are back, chattering over seeds.
All the snow's melted; the fruit trees are covered with downy new growth.
A few couples even walk in the meadow, promising whatever they promise.

We stand in the sun and the sun heals us.
It doesn't rush away. It hangs above us, unmoving,
like an actor pleased with his welcome.

My neighbor's quiet a moment,
staring at the mountain, listening to the birds.

So many garments, where did they come from?
And my neighbor's still out there,
fixing them to the line, as though the basket would never be empty—

It's still full, nothing is finished,
though the sun's beginning to move lower in the sky;
remember, it isn't summer yet, only the beginning of spring;
warmth hasn't taken hold yet, and the cold's returning—

She feels it, as though the last bit of linen had frozen in her hands.
She looks at her hands—how old they are. It's not the beginning, it's the end.
And the adults, they're all dead now.
Only the children are left, alone, growing old.

BURNING LEAVES

The dead leaves catch fire quickly.
And they burn quickly; in no time at all,
they change from something to nothing.

Midday. The sky is cold, blue;
under the fire, there's gray earth.

How fast it all goes, how fast the smoke clears.
And where the pile of leaves was,
an emptiness that suddenly seems vast.

Across the road, a boy's watching.
He stays a long time, watching the leaves burn.
Maybe this is how you'll know when the earth is dead—
it will ignite.

CROSSROADS

My body, now that we will not be traveling together much longer
I begin to feel a new tenderness toward you, very raw and unfamiliar,
like what I remember of love when I was young—

love that was so often foolish in its objectives
but never in its choices, its intensities.
Too much demanded in advance, too much that could not be promised—

My soul has been so fearful, so violent:
forgive its brutality.
As though it were that soul, my hand moves over you cautiously,

not wishing to give offense
but eager, finally, to achieve expression as substance:

it is not the earth I will miss,
it is you I will miss.

BATS

Concerning death, one might observe
that those with authority to speak remain silent:
others force their way to the pulpit or
center stage—experience
being always preferable to theory, they are rarely
true clairvoyants, nor is conviction
the common aspect of insight. Look up into the night:
if distraction through the senses is the essence of life
what you see now appears to be a simulation of death, bats
whirling in darkness— But man knows
nothing of death. If how we behave is how you feel,
this is not what death is like, this is what life is like.
You too are blind. You too flail in darkness.
A terrible solitude surrounds all beings who
confront mortality. As Margulies says: death
terrifies us all into silence.

ABUNDANCE

A cool wind blows on summer evenings, stirring the wheat.
The wheat bends, the leaves of the peach trees
rustle in the night ahead.

In the dark, a boy's crossing the field:
for the first time, he's touched a girl
so he walks home a man, with a man's hungers.

Slowly the fruit ripens—
baskets and baskets from a single tree
so some rots every year
and for a few weeks there's too much:
before and after, nothing.

Between the rows of wheat
you can see the mice, flashing and scurrying
across the earth, though the wheat towers above them,
churning as the summer wind blows.

The moon is full. A strange sound
comes from the field—maybe the wind.

But for the mice it's a night like any summer night.
Fruit and grain: a time of abundance.
Nobody dies, nobody goes hungry.

No sound except the roar of the wheat.

MIDSUMMER

On nights like this we used to swim in the quarry,
the boys making up games requiring them to tear off the girls' clothes
and the girls cooperating, because they had new bodies since last summer
and they wanted to exhibit them, the brave ones
leaping off the high rocks—bodies crowding the water.

The nights were humid, still. The stone was cool and wet,
marble for graveyards, for buildings that we never saw,
buildings in cities far away.

On cloudy nights, you were blind. Those nights the rocks were dangerous,
but in another way it was all dangerous, that was what we were after.
The summer started. Then the boys and girls began to pair off
but always there were a few left at the end—sometimes they'd keep watch,
sometimes they'd pretend to go off with each other like the rest,
but what could they do there, in the woods? No one wanted to be them.
But they'd show up anyway, as though some night their luck would change,
fate would be a different fate.

At the beginning and at the end, though, we were all together.
After the evening chores, after the smaller children were in bed,
then we were free. Nobody said anything, but we knew the nights we'd meet
and the nights we wouldn't. Once or twice, at the end of summer,
we could see a baby was going to come out of all that kissing.

And for those two, it was terrible, as terrible as being alone.
The game was over. We'd sit on the rocks smoking cigarettes,
worrying about the ones who weren't there.

And then finally walk home through the fields,
because there was always work the next day.
And the next day, we were kids again, sitting on the front steps in the morning,
eating a peach. Just that, but it seemed an honor to have a mouth.
And then going to work, which meant helping out in the fields.

One boy worked for an old lady, building shelves.
The house was very old, maybe built when the mountain was built.

And then the day faded. We were dreaming, waiting for night.
Standing at the front door at twilight, watching the shadows lengthen.
And a voice in the kitchen was always complaining about the heat,
wanting the heat to break.

Then the heat broke, the night was clear.
And you thought of the boy or girl you'd be meeting later.
And you thought of walking into the woods and lying down,
practicing all those things you were learning in the water.
And though sometimes you couldn't see the person you were with,
there was no substitute for that person.

The summer night glowed; in the field, fireflies were glinting.
And for those who understood such things, the stars were sending messages:
You will leave the village where you were born
and in another country you'll become very rich, very powerful,
but always you will mourn something you left behind, even though you
    can't say what it was,
and eventually you will return to seek it.

THRESHING

The sky's light behind the mountain
though the sun is gone—this light
is like the sun's shadow, passing over the earth.

Before, when the sun was high,
you couldn't look at the sky or you'd go blind.
That time of day, the men don't work.
They lie in the shade, waiting, resting;
their undershirts are stained with sweat.

But under the trees it's cool,
like the flask of water that gets passed around.
A green awning's over their heads, blocking the sun.
No talk, just the leaves rustling in the heat,
the sound of the water moving from hand to hand.

This hour or two is the best time of day.
Not asleep, not awake, not drunk,
and the women far away
so that the day becomes suddenly calm, quiet and expansive,
without the women's turbulence.

The men lie under their canopy, apart from the heat,
as though the work were done.
Beyond the fields, the river's soundless, motionless—
scum mottles the surface.

To a man, they know when the hour's gone.
The flask gets put away, the bread, if there's bread.
The leaves darken a little, the shadows change.
The sun's moving again, taking the men along,
regardless of their preferences.

Above the fields, the heat's fierce still, even in decline.
The machines stand where they were left,
patient, waiting for the men's return.

The sky's bright, but twilight is coming.
The wheat has to be threshed; many hours remain
before the work is finished.
And afterward, walking home through the fields,
dealing with the evening.

So much time best forgotten.
Tense, unable to sleep, the woman's soft body
always shifting closer—
That time in the woods: that was reality.
This is the dream.

The death and uncertainty that await me
as they await all men, the shadows evaluating me
because it can take time to destroy a human being,
the element of suspense
needs to be preserved—

On Sundays I walk my neighbor's dog
so she can go to church to pray for her sick mother.

The dog waits for me in the doorway. Summer and winter
we walk the same road, early morning, at the base of the escarpment.
Sometimes the dog gets away from me—for a moment or two,
I can't see him behind some trees. He's very proud of this,
this trick he brings out occasionally, and gives up again
as a favor to me—

Afterward, I go back to my house to gather firewood.

I keep in my mind images from each walk:
monarda growing by the roadside;
in early spring, the dog chasing the little gray mice,

so for a while it seems possible
not to think of the hold of the body weakening, the ratio
of the body to the void shifting,

and the prayers becoming prayers for the dead.

Midday, the church bells finished. Light in excess:
still, fog blankets the meadow, so you can't see
the mountain in the distance, covered with snow and ice.

When it appears again, my neighbor thinks
her prayers are answered. So much light she can't control her happiness—
it has to burst out in language. *Hello*, she yells, as though
that is her best translation.

She believes in the Virgin the way I believe in the mountain,
though in one case the fog never lifts.
But each person stores his hope in a different place.

I make my soup, I pour my glass of wine.
I'm tense, like a child approaching adolescence.
Soon it will be decided for certain what you are,
one thing, a boy or girl. Not both any longer.
And the child thinks: I want to have a say in what happens.
But the child has no say whatsoever.

When I was a child, I did not foresee this.

Later, the sun sets, the shadows gather,
rustling the low bushes like animals just awake for the night.
Inside, there's only firelight. It fades slowly;
now only the heaviest wood's still
flickering across the shelves of instruments.
I hear music coming from them sometimes,
even locked in their cases.

When I was a bird, I believed I would be a man.
That's the flute. And the horn answers,
when I was a man, I cried out to be a bird.
Then the music vanishes. And the secret it confides in me
vanishes also.

In the window, the moon is hanging over the earth,
meaningless but full of messages.

It's dead, it's always been dead,
but it pretends to be something else,
burning like a star, and convincingly, so that you feel sometimes
it could actually make something grow on earth.

If there's an image of the soul, I think that's what it is.

I move through the dark as though it were natural to me,
as though I were already a factor in it.
Tranquil and still, the day dawns.
On market day, I go to the market with my lettuces.

Note

The second "Bats" is dedicated to Ellen Pinsky. The last sentence appears in a paper written by Alfred Margulies, MD, presented at the Massachusetts School of Professional Psychology, March 5, 1998.